BigTime® Piano

Hits

Level 4

Intermediate

Arranged by

Randall Faber and Jon Ophoff

Special Thanks to Christopher Oill
Editor: Isabel Otero Bowen
Design and Illustration: Terpstra Design, San Francisco
Engraving: Dovetree Productions, Inc.

FABER
PIANO ADVENTURES®
3042 Creek Drive
Ann Arbor, Michigan 48108

A NOTE TO TEACHERS

BigTime® Piano Hits is a collection of popular songs arranged for the intermediate piano student. Enjoy blockbusters, chart-toppers, and award-winners as performed by stars such as Bruno Mars, Katy Perry, Justin Bieber, Taylor Swift, and more.

BigTime® Piano Hits is part of the *BigTime Piano* series arranged by Faber and Faber. As the name implies, this level marks a significant achievement for the piano student.

Following are the levels of the supplementary library, which lead from *PreTime* to *BigTime*.

PreTime® Piano	(Primer Level)
PlayTime® Piano	(Level 1)
ShowTime® Piano	(Level 2A)
ChordTime® Piano	(Level 2B)
FunTime® Piano	(Level 3A–3B)
BigTime® Piano	(Level 4)

Each level offers books in a variety of styles, making it possible for the teacher to offer stimulating material for every student. For a complimentary detailed listing, e-mail faber@pianoadventures.com or write us at the mailing address below.

Visit us at **PianoAdventures.com**.

Helpful Hints:

1. The songs can be assigned in any order. Selection is usually best made by the student, according to interest and enthusiasm.

2. As rhythm is of prime importance, encourage the student to feel the rhythm in his or her body when playing popular music. This can be accomplished with the tapping of the toe or heel, and with clapping exercises.

3. Chord symbols are given above the treble staff. Time taken to help the student see how chords are used in the arrangement is time well spent. Such work can help memory, sightreading, and the development of improvisation, composition, and arranging skills.

ISBN 978-1-61677-696-1

FF3037

TABLE OF CONTENTS

Hello. 4

See You Again. 7

What About Us 10

Sugar 13

Firework. 16

When I Was Your Man 19

Sorry, , , , ...22

Stay With Me. 25

Symphony 28

All of Me 32

Shake It Off 35

Shut Up and Dance 38

Music Dictionary 41

FF3037

Hello

Words and Music by ADELE ADKINS
and GREG KURSTIN

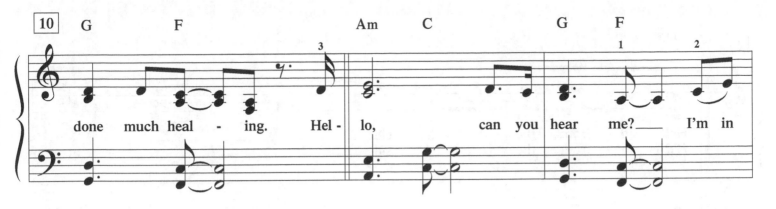

done much heal - ing. Hel - lo, can you hear me?___ I'm in

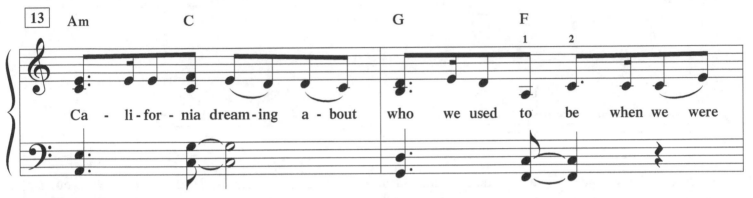

Ca - li - for - nia dream - ing a - bout who we used to be when we were

young-er___ and free.___ I've for - got - ten how it felt be - fore the

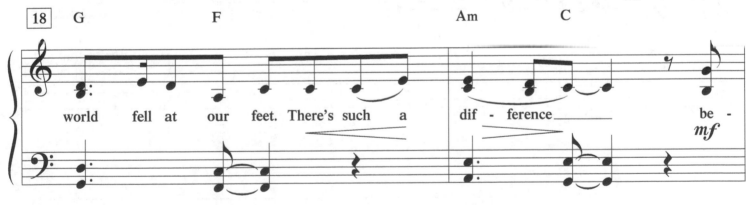

world fell at our feet. There's such a dif - ference___ be -

tween___ us___ and a mil - lion___ miles.

See You Again

Words and Music by CAMERON THOMAZ,
CHARLIE PUTH, JUSTIN FRANKS, ANDREW CEDAR,
DANN HUME, JOSH HARDY and PHOEBE COCKBURN

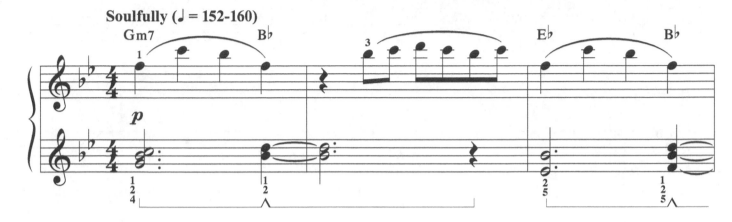

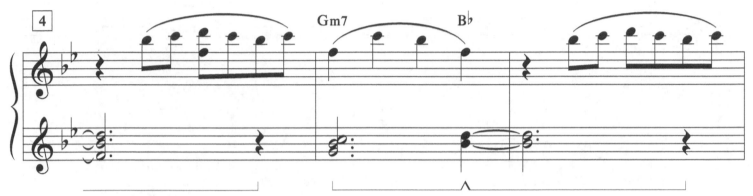

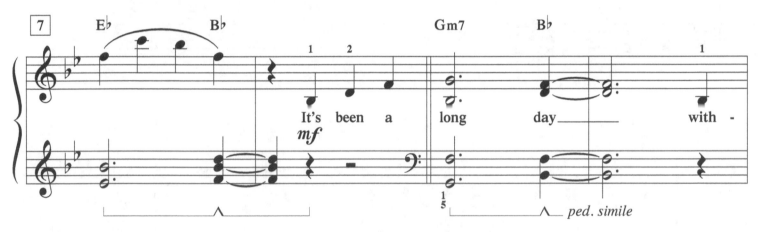

see you a - gain.___ We've come a long way___ from

where we be - gan.___ Oh, I'll tell you all a - bout it when I

see you a - gain.___ When I see you a - gain.

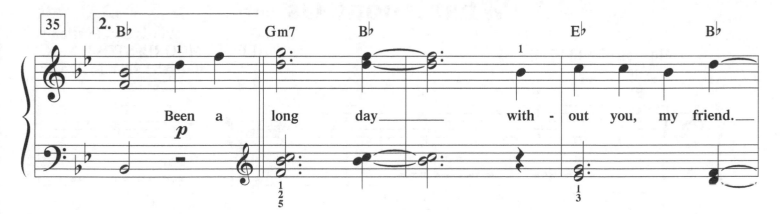

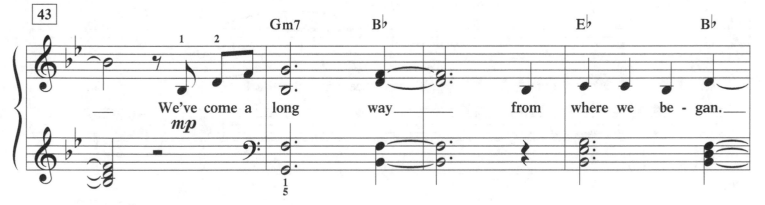

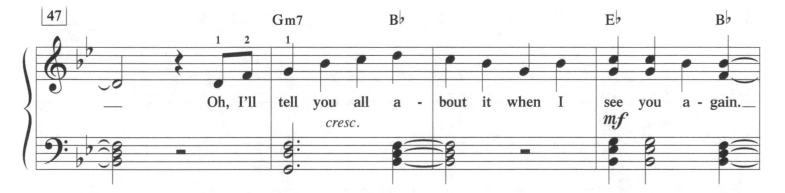

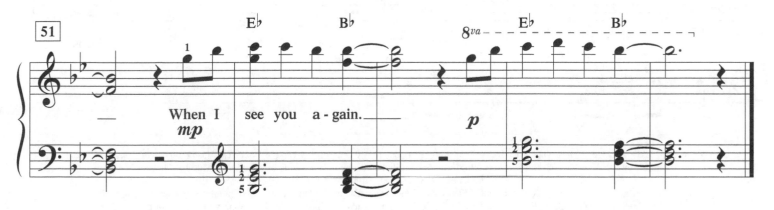

What About Us

Words and Music by
ALECIA MOORE, STEVE MAC
and JOHNNY McDAID

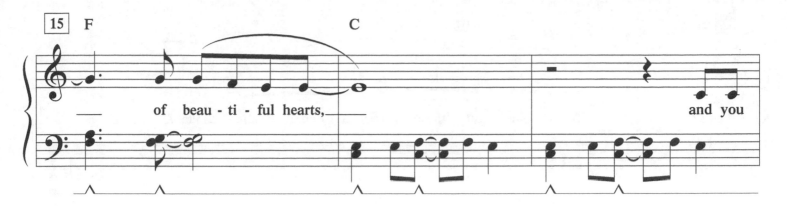

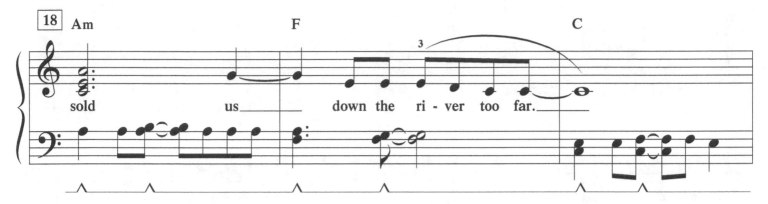

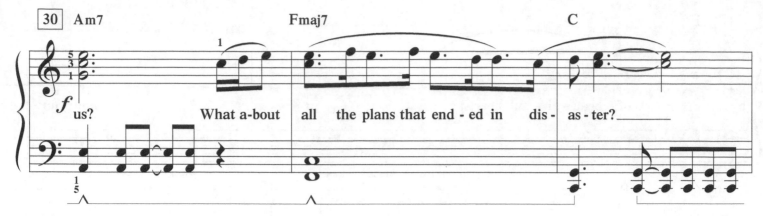

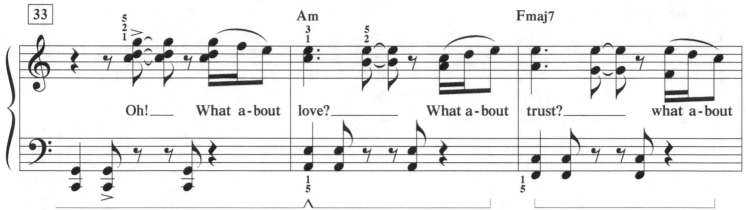

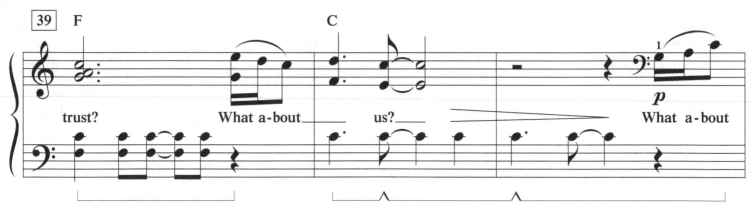

Sugar

Words and Music by ADAM LEVINE,
HENRY WALTER, JOSHUA COLEMAN, LUKASZ GOTTWALD,
JACOB KASHER HINDLIN and MIKE POSNER

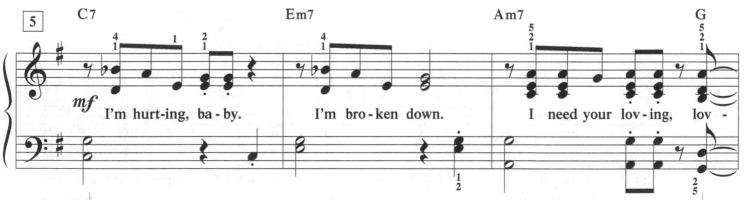

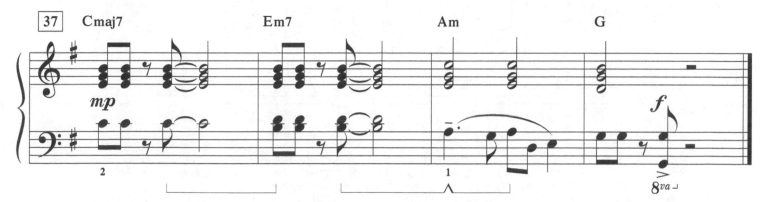

Firework

Words and Music by KATY PERRY,
MIKKEL ERIKSEN, TOR ERIK HERMANSEN,
ESTHER DEAN and SANDY WILHELM

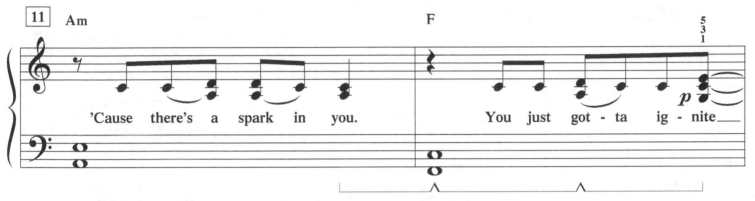

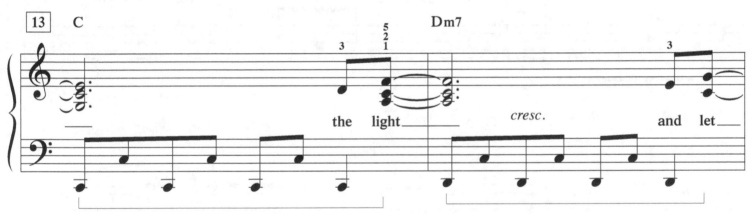

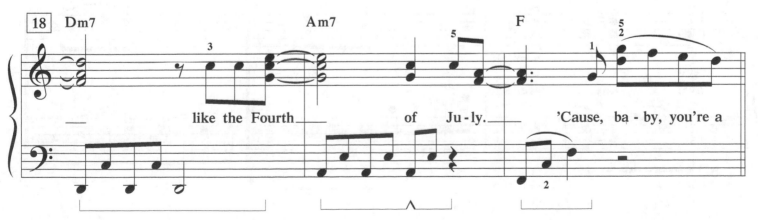

18

When I Was Your Man

Words and Music by BRUNO MARS,
ARI LEVINE, PHILIP LAWRENCE and ANDREW WYATT

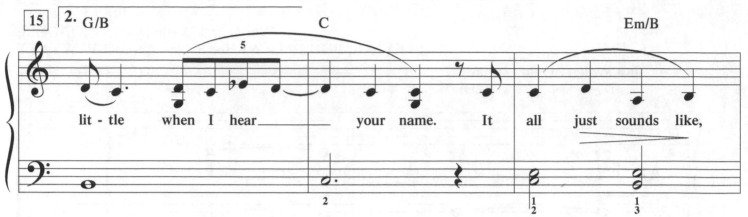

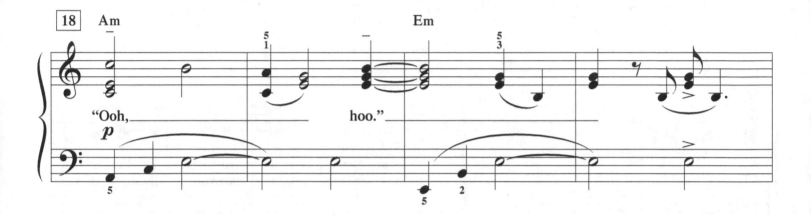

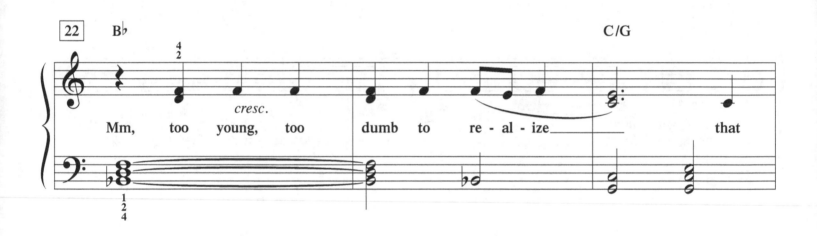

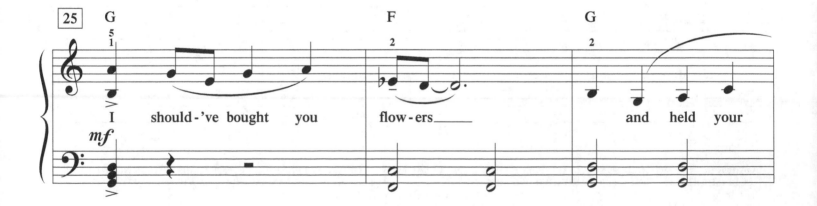

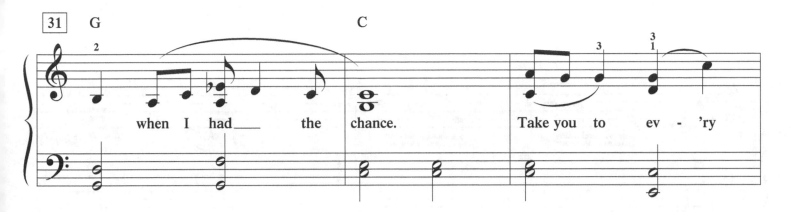

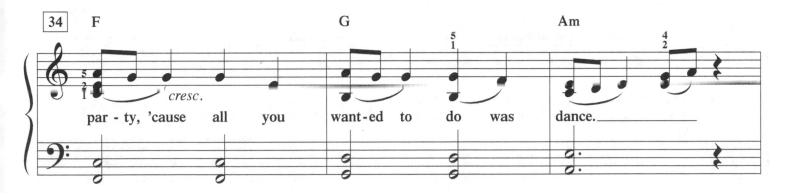

Sorry

Words and Music by JUSTIN BIEBER,
SONNY MOORE, MICHAEL TUCKER,
JULIA MICHAELS, and JUSTIN TRANTER

Steady beat (♩ = 96–100)

You got-ta go and get an-gry at all of my hones-ty.
You know you know that I made those mis-takes may-be once or twice.

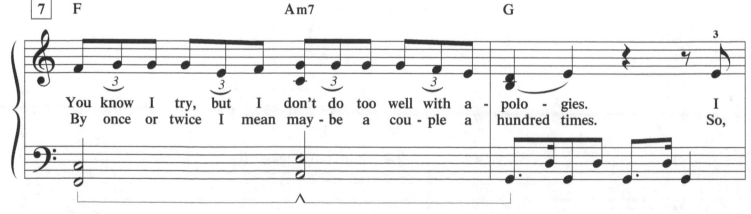

You know I try, but I don't do too well with a-polo-gies.
By once or twice I mean may-be a cou-ple a hundred times.

FF3037

know, oh,___ that I let you down. Is it too late___ to say I'm sor - ry now?

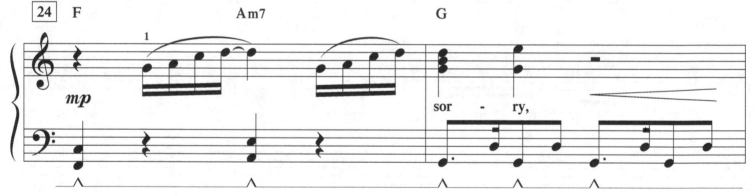

Sor - ry,

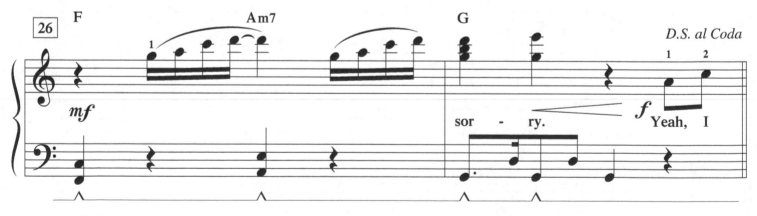

sor - ry,

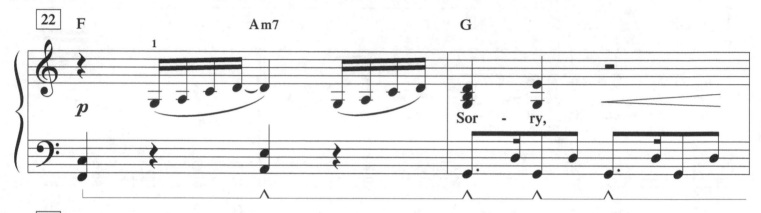

sor - ry. Yeah, I

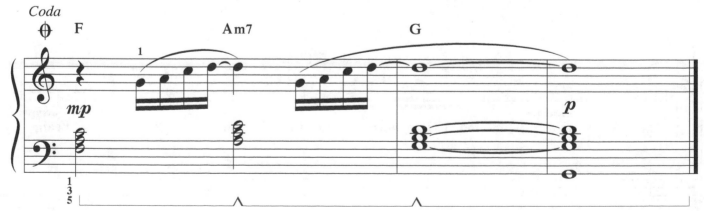

Stay With Me

Words and Music by SAM SMITH,
JAMES NAPIER, WILLIAM EDWARD PHILLIPS,
TOM PETTY and JEFF LYNNE

FF3037

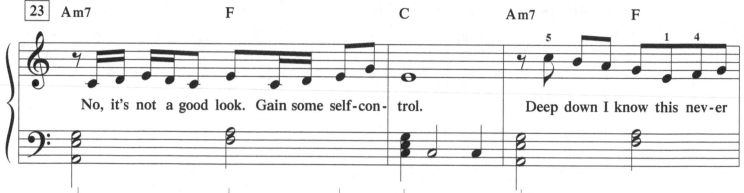

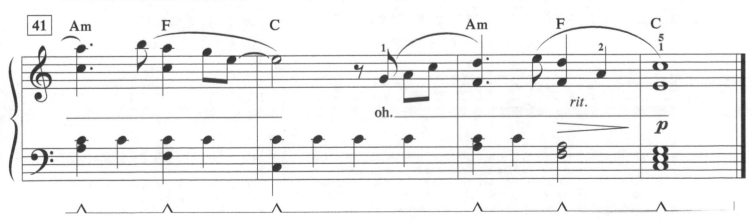

Symphony

Words and Music by JACK PATTERSON,
INA WROLDSEN, STEVE MAC
and AMMAR MALIK

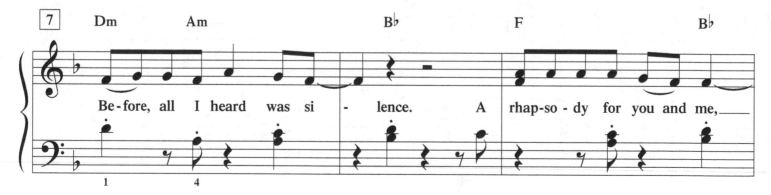

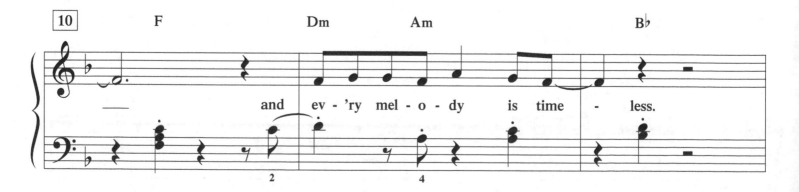

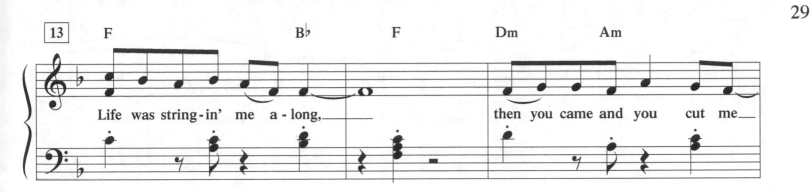

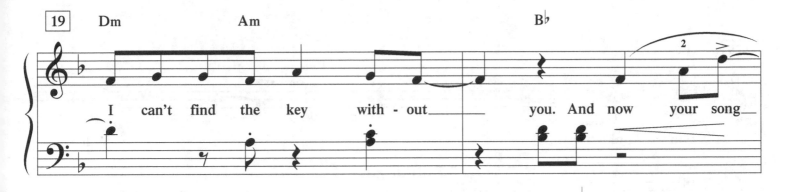

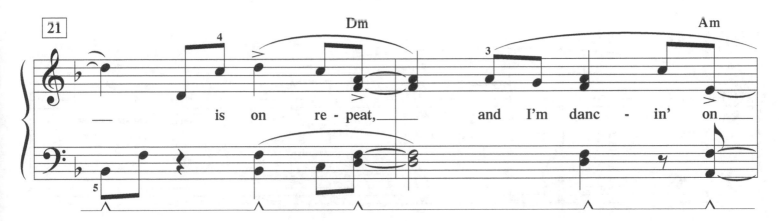

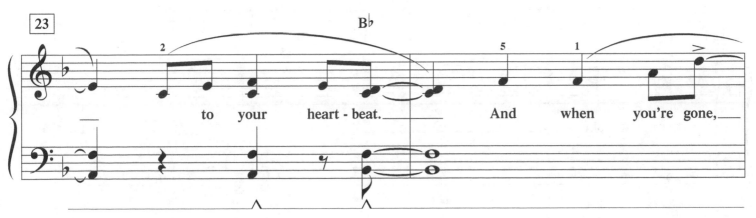

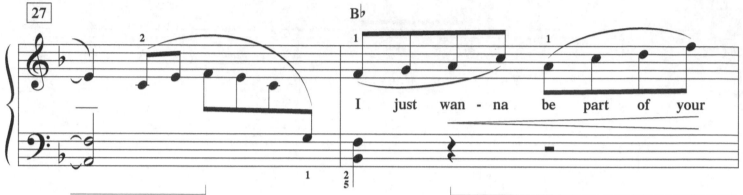

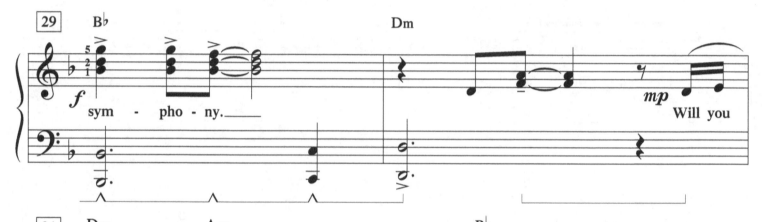

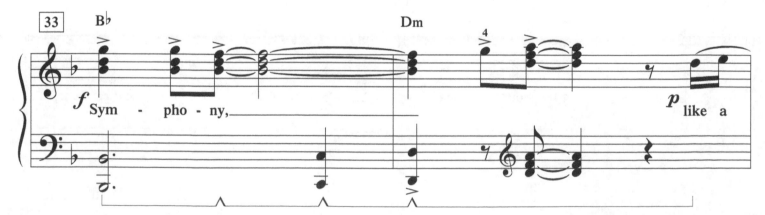

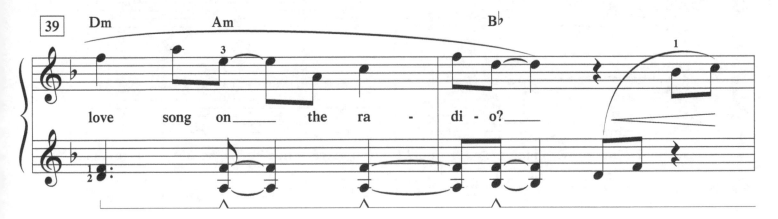

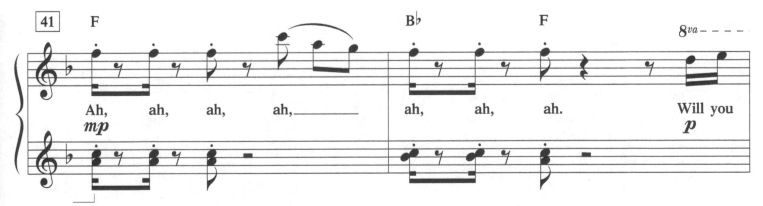

All of Me

Words and Music by JOHN STEPHENS
and TOBY GAD

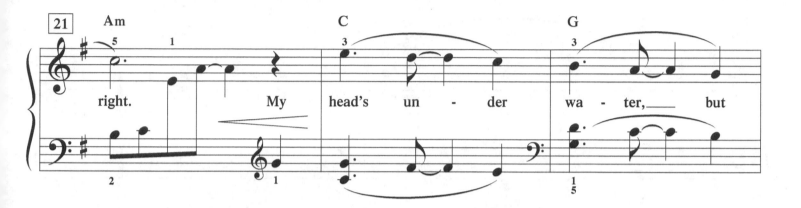

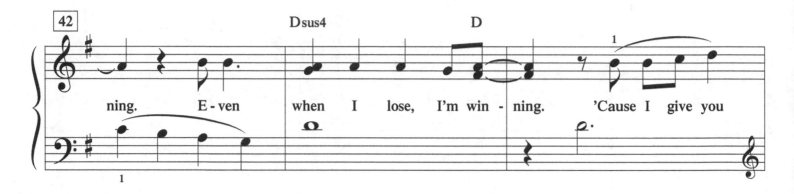

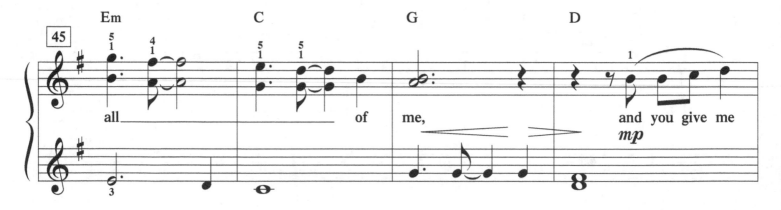

Shake It Off

Words and Music by TAYLOR SWIFT,
MAX MARTIN and SHELLBACK

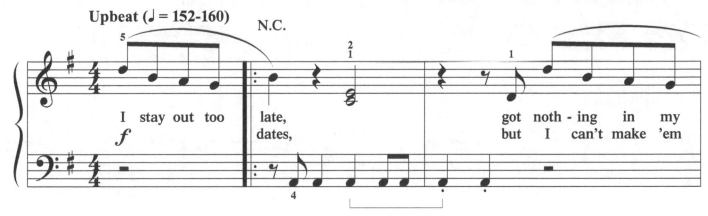

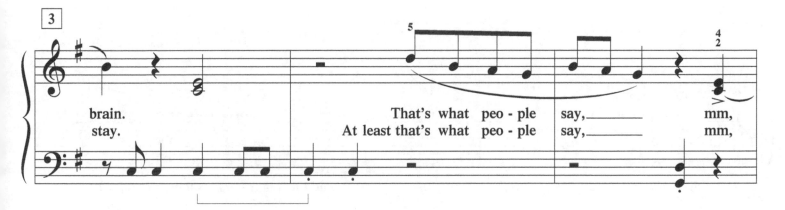

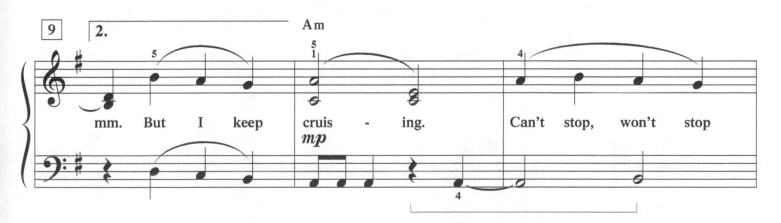

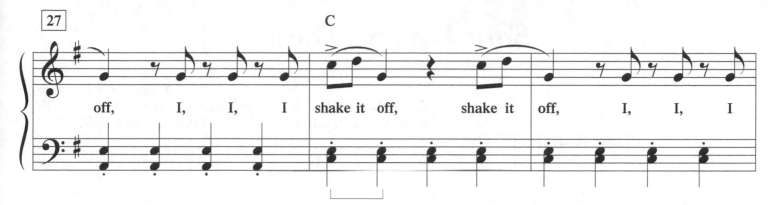

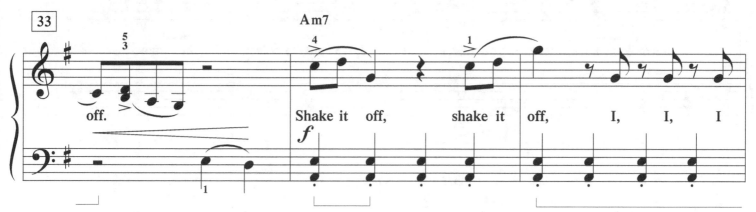

Shut Up and Dance

Words and Music by
RYAN McMAHON, BEN BERGER, SEAN WAUGAMAN,
ELI MAIMAN, NICHOLAS PETRICCA and KEVIN RAY

We were victims of the night. Chem - i - cal,__ phy - si - cal, kryp - ton - ite.

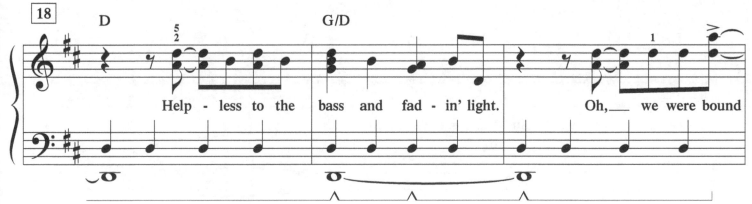

Help - less to the bass and fad - in' light. Oh,__ we were bound

__ to get to - geth - er, bound __ to get to - geth - er. She took my arm

I don't know how it hap - pened. We took the floor and she said,__ "Oh, don't you

27 | D | G/D | A/D | D | G/D

dare look back, just keep your eyes on me." I said, "You're hold-in' back." She said, "Shut

30 | Bm7 | A | D | G/D | D

up and dance with me." This wom-an is my des-tin-y. She said,

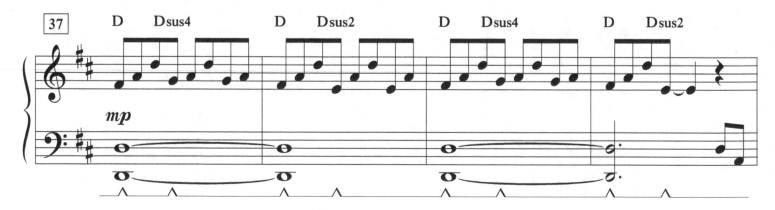

33 | D/F♯ | G | D/F♯ | A | G

"Ooh___ hoo, shut up and dance with me."

p

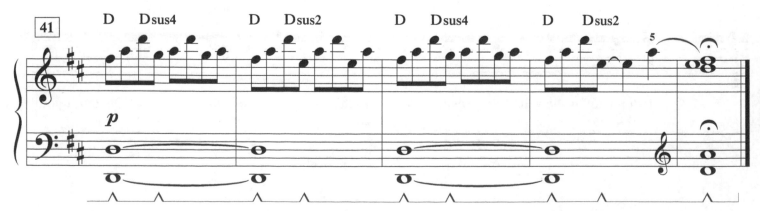

37 | D | Dsus4 | D | Dsus2 | D | Dsus4 | D | Dsus2

mp

41 | D | Dsus4 | D | Dsus2 | D | Dsus4 | D | Dsus2

p